LIVING THE DREAM

A GOOD LIFE WSTED IN THE GREAT OUTDOORS

TIMOTHY E. TIPTON

DEDICATION

This book is for several people in my family.

For my kids, Taylor and Cody, who raised me as much as I raised them, and for always following your mom's example.

My grandkids Zackery, Zianna, Laney, Asher (Bubs) and Aiden. Here's to you having fulfilling lives. May you always have clean air and pure water to enjoy the outdoors.

Special thanks to my wife of 35 years, Jennifer. Your love and support have always been a blessing and have kept my life mostly on track. Thank you for everything you do for us. Without you, none of this would be possible. I love you.

TABLE OF CONTENTS

INTRODUCTION

Just before I left to go to a fly fishing guide school in Montana, I signed up for an email list that keeps you updated on guide job openings in the United States, and Canada

The Rocky Mountain west intrigued me, and working in Alaska was pure romance, I needed to be a realist. I had a young grandson who was going to have a little sister in a few months. I needed to be within reasonable driving distance of home. We also needed to be in a place where my wife, a Registered Nurse, could find work as a travel nurse. Things all came together perfectly through one email from the guide jobs page. There was a guide service that had a need for more guides, and they were based in the Smoky Mountains.

I have been going to the Smokies since I was a child. When I started fly fishing, my wife, kids, and I would go there at least once a year and sometimes more. I would wake up early and get four or five hours of fishing in, get back to camp or the hotel, depending on our chosen accommodations, and the family would be ready to do tourist things. I knew the park and its fishing well, and it was only a four-and-a-half-hour drive from home.

Before I left for Montana, I called the number of the guide service and left a voicemail for the owner. He called me back later in the day and we talked for about 15 minutes. It sounded promising, and he told me to call him back after I returned from Montana.

When I returned home from guide school in mid-March, I called the owner of the guide service again. I got voicemail once more, which disappointed me, but I left a message anyway. Later in the afternoon, I went to buy a part for my wife's car. While I was getting ready to walk into the auto parts store, I received a phone call that would change my immediate future. It was the owner of the guide service calling me. We conducted a 30-minute interview, and he offered me my first job as a genuine fly fishing guide in the Smoky Mountains, all while sitting in the parking lot of the local AutoZone. Filled with excitement, I wasted no time and drove straight home to inform my wife. I didn't even go inside the store to get the part I needed. I would have to come back later.

The good news about guiding in the Great Smoky Mountains National Park (GSMNP) was that I had 20 years of experience fishing here. The bad news was those years added up to about 6-to-10 days a year. I knew the park and its fishing, but I really didn't know it the way I needed to take paying clients. Drawing from my experience of writing about and sharing a boat with elite professional bass tournament anglers, I formulated a plan. I would practice on these streams like a tournament pro practiced during the official practice periods.

Each morning, I began driving to the park. Driving along a lot of the streams. I would use pull outs along the water, get out and make a few casts in various pools. Using a size twelve dry fly with the hook removed, I was looking for bites. Every time I found a pool where I got a lot of action, I would mark it on my GPS. It worked. When I could finally start taking my own clients, I was confident because I had many spots I could take them. Being confident in yourself is important when dealing with clients and this pre-fishing I had done really paid off.

I also felt at home in the Smokies. There seemed to be a spiritual connection between me and these mountains. Eventually, I would realize why.

These southern Appalachians felt like home to me. I've never lived here, but there is a powerful family and spiritual bond when I am here.

My roots are in these mountains. My ancestors lived in the mountains of Cherokee, NC, and Cades Cove in Tennessee. They worked in the coal mines of eastern Kentucky, Virginia, and West Virginia. They had names of Patton, Davis, Tipton, and Haynes, among others. I always feel a sense of home when I am in these mountains. It also helps to comfort me to know these mountains are full of bear, deer, turkey, and most of all, wild trout.

So, I became a fly fishing guide. Something I would not have thought of back in the days of my youth. Still, I wouldn't have traded these experiences for the world. Getting to work in the Smokies each day was a treat. The opportunity to teach newcomers about the sport was a pure joy. Sometimes, when driving in to or out of the park during a workday, I would pull off the road and stare out at some of the gorgeous views that the park offers. It never got old.

Through this job, I got to experience things that I never would have experienced before, when I was just a tourist. Unintentionally, I was within ten feet of a rather large male black bear and learned about their strong smell up close. I've had the opportunity to observe mother bears with their offspring. I've seen large, majestic whitetail bucks. Myself and two clients witnessed a doe with triplet fawns, and one magical afternoon, my clients and I observed a doe giving birth in a field from afar. I've had elk come down to the water and ignore us, as they walked in the river to drink.

In the fall of 2016, I watched as fire raged through my beloved National Park and devastated the town of Gatlinburg. I also watched the strength and resilience of these mountain people as they banded together to rebuild.

Besides my love of the mountains, I have learned to appreciate the people here. Their accents, their southern hospitality, and their overall kindness. I made good friends here that I keep in touch with and visit when I'm in the area.

Though I no longer live here, I still consider it my home. Kids and grandchildren beckoned me home to Kentucky. Perhaps, when the grandkids get older, I will return to full-time Smokey Mountain living. Until that time, I will continue to visit, and reminisce about my time spent here.

I've also experienced some humorous things. Some of these stories are told here. In most cases, I have changed names to protect the identity of some folks involved. These stories are true to the best of my memory, which can be cloudy at best.

Not all these stories involve fly fishing in the Smoky Mountains. Some are about fly fishing in other areas. Some are about my love of traditional archery and bow hunting. I hope you enjoy them. I know I sure enjoyed living this dream and telling these stories in print.

Tim Tipton
Townsend, TN

CHAPTER 1
NEW BEGINNINGS

I was in the middle of Illinois when I asked myself, "Are you sure you want to do this?" After nearly four hours alone on the road, I was feeling some trepidation. On this solitary journey, I was traveling by car from my Shepherdsville, Kentucky home, to Fort Smith, Montana, to chase a nearly 20-year dream, but now I was having second thoughts. It would be a long, lonely two-day drive, at the end of which would be the Bighorn Angler Lodge and Fly Shop near the famous trout river of the same name, and a week of learning the ins and outs of being a fly-fishing guide.

Allow me to backtrack to the late-90's. I was a married father of two young children, working as a sports editor for a small-town newspaper, taking a few college courses, trying to make a few dollars as a freelance writer and punishing my liver each day for some unknown crime.

I had just officially "retired" from a mediocre career as a professional boxer, in which I took way too many punches, for way too little pay. The result being a severely deviated septum, a steel plate screwed into my jaw, and a case of arthritis that occasionally flares up in my right hand. My only real hobbies were fishing and hunting, something I had done for most of my life.

In 1998, I went on my first guided fly-fishing trip on the Hiwassee River in Tennessee. It was an assignment for a magazine. When the editor says go, you go. If someone wants to pay you to go on a fishing trip, you do it. It's tough, but necessary.

1

I had been fly fishing intermittently for a couple of years, but this would be different. It was on a large tailwater, and I would fish in a drift boat for the first time. It was also my first experience fly-fishing with an expert (anyone that knew more than me about fly fishing was an expert in my book).

By the day's end, my casting stroke had improved, I caught more trout than I would normally catch in a week, was well fed, and had sky-high confidence in my ability to catch fish on a fly. Returning home, I was eager to put into practice what I had learned and see if it worked in my fishing spots. I also came home with a thought gnawing at the back of my mind; I wanted to be a fly fishing guide. Of course, this was a pipe dream. I was 31 years old with a family, a job and all the responsibilities that come with adulthood. However, the thought lingered in the back of my mind.

Fast forward 18 years. My daughter is married with a child, my son has just moved out on his own and I am unemployed. One afternoon on a whim, I googled fly fishing guide schools and the first thing that popped up was an article in Field & Stream by Ted Leeson. In the piece, Leeson attends the Sweetwater Travel Company Guide School in Montana. The article was a well-written account of how the guide school operates and the type of people that attend. I immediately decided that Sweetwater was where I needed to be. After all, it was good enough for Leeson, and I owned some of his books, so this must be the right place.

My wife questioned my sanity because I was driving instead of flying. Flying is not something I enjoy. I've done it just enough to not be terrified, but also just enough to know my travel plans are at the mercy of someone else. I told her it would be fine; that I enjoyed my company. Just two hours into this long drive I thought about that statement and realized, "Tim, you really aren't as interesting as you believed."

So, I was on the road for a solitary two-day drive. I traveled north on interstate 65 to Indianapolis, onto Interstate 74 across Illinois, and over the Mississippi River to Davenport, Iowa. I then hit Interstate 80 and finally, around sundown, I stopped for the night near Cedar Rapids. A nice hot shower and a good night's sleep felt extravagant after the day on the road.

Up early the next morning, I bolted breakfast and coffee and jumped back on the highway, taking Interstate 380 northwest to Interstate 29 in Sioux Falls, South Dakota. I stopped in a rest area for a bathroom break, only to witness two men punching each other in the face in the parking lot. The conflict broke up shortly, and each went on their way. I am not sure what the skirmish was about, or who the winner was---if there was one. Regardless, I needed the restroom.

The drive across South Dakota provided views of pine-covered hills, rolling prairies, and red-walled canyons through the windshield. I would have loved to stop and see Devil's Tower and other landmarks. Unfortunately, there was no time. The state had one downfall. I could only pick up a few radio stations, and each one was carrying the same political talk show.

Interstate 90 was the last Interstate I would travel on my journey. I had planned on arriving at the lodge that night, but darkness and fatigue won out. Falling short of my goal, I ended up in a motel in Sheridan, Wyoming, just short of the Montana border.

Early the next morning, I had three cups of coffee and enjoyed two trips through the continental breakfast before I finished the last ninety minutes of my trip. There would be a minor blunder along the way.

I have a nasty habit involving chewing loose leaf tobacco. I've quit several times, but then my willpower breaks, and I am back at it. It is especially prevalent when I am driving. That morning, I stopped at a gas station/grocery store on the Crow Agency Reservation to top off the tank and purchase a few packs of my favorite chewing tobacco. After getting my gas, I entered the store, where a Native American man around my age was stocking shelves. The man was in the six feet range, slender with medium length, jet black hair, piercing dark eyes and high cheekbones. Behind the counter was a native American woman working the register. It was then when the country bumpkin in me rose to the surface. I walked up to the counter and asked the woman, "do you have Red Man?" She glared at me, and the gentleman stopped his work and gave me the side eye. At that distinct sound of silence, I realized what I had done. I immediately apologized, reached in my back pocket, pulled out a half-filled pouch of Red Man chewing tobacco, and showed it to the man and woman. They soon erupted into deep laughter, and I was off the hook for the misunderstanding. I may have been off the hook, but unfortunately, they didn't carry that brand for understandable reasons.

Upon arriving at the lodge that morning, I wasn't sure where I was supposed to check in. I walked into the fly shop, which seemed like the obvious place to get information. I met Ron Meek, the director of the guide school. He gave me my room key, told me that our first day of instruction would begin at one p.m. and left me to my own devices. After unpacking and settling in my room, I decided to have a look around. First, it was back to the fly shop to buy a Montana fishing license and browse. Then it was on to the river, just a couple of minutes from the Bighorn Angler. I stopped at the boat launch area at the Yellowtail Dam at Bighorn Canyon.

Here, the Bighorn River flows through an open and isolated landscape. I had done most of my fly fishing on small woodland streams, and the Bighorn was much different. The river sits on the edge of the plains, with very few trees except along the riverbank, where numerous cottonwoods and brush line the river's edge. The Pryor Mountains and the lesser Bighorn Mountains jut up from the plains in the distance, providing a scenic background from the river.

Construction of the Yellowtail Dam took place in the 1960s. They built the dam for flood control, hydroelectricity, and irrigation, but it also created one of the finest tailwater fisheries in the United States. One thing I learned over the next six days was that there were about 6,000 trout per mile in the upper 13 miles of the Bighorn River, but just because they're in there doesn't mean they are easy to catch.

When we assembled in the meeting room/dining room that afternoon, one thing struck me immediately; I was by far the oldest one in the class. Apart from three students, most were college kids on spring break. In other words, they were in the same age group as my own kids.

It was an eclectic group. We had two high school kids, that were brother and sister. They had as much experience in fly fishing as any of us students, despite their young age. They were from somewhere in the New England area but had fished many times in Montana. One of my roommates was Harrison, who lived across the border in Wyoming. He had been in the Marine Corps and had done time in the second Gulf War. My other roommate lived a couple of hours away in Montana, who was also one of the three students in my boating group. The other student in our boating group was Rob, a college student from Ole Miss, who enjoyed talking sports and showed up one morning with an extreme hangover. There was also Max. Max had a long, sandy blonde beard and long hair. This was before long beards became cliché, and he wore them well. He was a silent and somewhat serious young man. I was never in the boat with Max, but from reports I got, he was a fish-catching machine.

The two students that I spent the most time talking with were Eric and Jordan. They were a little closer to my age, and we hit it off well. They had driven to Montana from Pennsylvania and were avid fly fisherman. Eric was a mechanic who worked on Harley Davidson's. Jordan was a former mixed martial arts fighter and coach, and a fan of the Grateful Dead. The day we left Montana, I would run into them at a rest area in South Dakota, where I had stopped to stretch my legs and use the restroom. A few months later, me and Jordan would end up working for the same outfitter in the Smokies.

Our first class that day was fly tying. I thought I should have an advantage over the other students in this area. I was the only one who had his own vise, and I had been tying for years, even if I was an unexceptional tier. As it turns out, I was wrong. I forgot that folks in their 20s have better eyesight, dexterity, and hand/eye coordination. Something I should have recalled from my days in a boxing ring. After four hours of tying various fly patterns, we had dinner and got to know each other over a few cold beers.

They divided us into groups of three, along with an instructor. The curriculum differed from what you may think. The instructors, who were all experienced guides, were not present to teach you how to fly fish. If you're interested in guiding, it's assumed you know how to fish. Instead, the focus was on teaching you how to deal with clients, make good decisions, provide casting instruction, handle the boat properly, tie knots, and read water.

We spent most days on boating instruction. If you have never done it, rowing a drift boat is much more difficult than you can imagine. In the hands of a skilled oarsman, it seems simple. With a 48-year-old grandfather fighting a stiff Montana breeze, it was quite the opposite.

The first thing you must get used to is rowing backwards. As someone who has paddled canoes and kayaks for years, this was completely foreign to me. Even more confusing was the method of rowing to avoid running into things. In most watercraft, you turn away from the obstruction. In a drift boat, you turn the bow of the watercraft toward the object and back row. Once you get the hang of this, it makes perfect sense, but it is a little frightening at first.

We also spent time learning to maintain and operate a jet boat, which I was much more comfortable with. I had spent most of my life operating motorboats, even before I was old enough to drive a car, so the tiller-steer jet boat was vaguely familiar. I excelled at this and enjoyed sliding through bends in the river like a dirt track race car driver. In fact, I felt so comfortable driving the jet boat that I opted to go out in it again on my last day.

We also learned the ins and outs of teaching fly casting from Brant Oswald. Oswald has over 30 years' experience as a guide and casting instructor who specializes in teaching casting and guiding on Montana's spring creeks and tailwaters. He served as an advisor on set for the Robert Redford-directed A River Runs Through It and to watch him lay out a perfect cast repeatedly can be quite intimidating when you know he is getting ready to watch your cast.

Our last class was a four-hour crash course in CPR and first aid. The class was helpful because many states require guides to be certified in these skills in case of emergency. A Livingston firefighter/EMT taught our course. He was a boisterous bundle of energy with a great sense of humor who made an uncomfortable subject enjoyable. Afterward, it was time to pack, do an exit interview and receive our diplomas.

As I drove out of the parking lot of the Bighorn Angler heading towards Hardin and the long drive home, I realized a big change in my life was on its way.

CHAPTER 2

HOW I GOT THIS WAY

"Fishing and hunting trips are not singular episodes. Instead, they are like chapters in a book. One chapter does not tell the entire story. These trips add up to one long adventure. If they were predictable, there would be no reason to go,"—Tim Tipton, Outdoor Sage, and Amateur Philosopher.

Unlike many longtime anglers, I can't recall the first fish I caught. I have my suspicions about it, but no solid memories float up to my commonly forgetful brain. I frequently rely on two excuses for this cognitive malfunction. Throughout my 16-year career as a boxer, I experienced repeated blows to the head, as an amateur and professional. Also, my brain, like the rest of me, is now solidly in its late-50s.

My wife, whom I've been married to for 35 years, says my long-term memory is surprisingly good, but I often forget things that happened yesterday. I can still remember the first time I kissed her goodnight on her parents' front porch in October 1987, but alas, I can't recall that first fish.

My best guess is that my first fish relates to one of my grandfathers. Both were avid anglers, but from opposite sides of the fishing spectrum. My grandpa Lawrence Tipton, who everyone knew as "Cactus," lived across the street from us in a rural, two-street subdivision in the small community of Brooks, Kentucky. One advantage of living so close was not only did we get to see him every day, but he also owned a pontoon boat, and a lake view lot on Rough River Lake, in the central part of the state.

Grandpa Tipton loved to fish, particularly if there were catfish involved. As kids, we spent a lot of time at Grandpa's camp, fishing, swimming, water skiing, playing badminton, volleyball, and the always exciting lawn darts. I miss lawn darts. Young people today will never know the thrill of dodging a sharp-edged projectile hurled through the air by a kid with little to no hand-eye coordination and only a vague notion of where the dart will land. Fortunately, none of us were ever seriously injured.

Grandpa would allow me to tag along on some of his early morn-ing fishing excursions. I was afforded this opportunity if I would get up early, stay quiet, keep out of the way, and bait my hook. I would accomplish most of the rules, but staying quiet was a problem. Most people that know me will tell you it is still difficult for me. They are not wrong.

My dad, also named Lawrence, but called Buddy, would sometimes join us. Other times, he would take us down to the water and let us fish off the back of the anchored pontoon. I could get in a lot of fishing, even though I didn't really know what I was doing much of the time.

I began serious fishing when I was around nineteen or twenty years old. My grandfather Patton, who I always called papaw, or papaw Tom, bought a small bass boat with a foot-operated trolling motor when he was in his seventies. Unfortunately for him, but fortunately for myself and a couple of other family members, he could not haul the boat and could never get the hang of the trolling motor.

We would fish many reservoirs within a two-hour drive. We learned to use baitcasting reels and throw artificial lures for largemouth and smallmouth bass. In addition, we engaged in fishing for various types of fish and took pleasure in catching any we could lure to bite. But bass were our passion. We became members of B.A.S.S. and read Bassmaster from cover to cover every month. Between the two of us, we acquired the latest and greatest lures. My cousin Scott, a pro bass angler and fishing guide, sold us second-hand fishing rods and reels. We also picked his brain about the newest lures and techniques. We never became experts, but we got competent at catching bass.

It was around this time in my life that fly fishing creeped into my thoughts. I was working at a newspaper covering sports; something that had begun as a dream. I was working and helping my wife as we raised two young children, but I wasn't fishing much. I still saw papaw or talked to him by phone nearly every day. During a stretch of this time, he even lived with us. Unfortunately, it was physically taxing on him every time we fished, so trips were few. Most of the fishing I was doing now was on a stream near my office at the newspaper. Smallmouth bass inhabited the stream, and they stocked rainbow trout during certain times of the year. I bought a pair of cheap waders and a light action spinning rod and reel. I would hit the creek tossing small soft plastic baits, and little hard bodied crankbaits. This usually resulted in a lot of small fish, which were a lot of fun, but there was something missing.

I bought my first fly rod on a whim. I was in the old Fischer's Sporting Goods store in Shepherdsville, talking to one of the two brothers that owned the place, while idly surveying products. My thirty-first birthday had recently come and gone, and I was in town, killing time before heading to the office.

I had taken an interest in fly fishing; even took a try at casting my uncle's fly rod in his yard. I still hadn't bought my first fly rod, but I was ready to pull the trigger. While browsing the store inventory, searching for anything that might strike my fancy, I came upon a cheap fly rod and reel, complete with backing and six-weight floating fly line. I paid thirty dollars for the entire setup. There was no doubt the quality was poor; a company that was well known for making bowling equipment made the rod. My guess is this was their first time venturing into the fly fishing market. Hopefully, it was their last foray.

The rod was serviceable, or at least, that's how I would have described it back then. What I now know, thirty years later, is that it was a genuine piece of crap. It was like casting a broom handle, except it was less flexible. I learned to cast with it, thanks to a quick lesson in the parking lot of an old fly shop. A gentleman named Norman Wathen taught me a basic cast in a matter of five minutes. I remember watching his smooth stroke as he laid out perfect casts one after another. He then handed me the rod back and said, "son, when you have a little money, you really need a better rod." I eventually bought a better rod, along with other gear, from the fly shop where Norman worked.

I took that rod to a 25-acre lake in a public forest area near home. This lake fishes well in the spring. Once the summer heat arrives, the lake is choked with weeds and grass and almost impossible to fish. It holds lots of bluegills and other panfish, and a generous population of bass in the one-to-two-pound range. My first fish on a fly rod was a largemouth bass around ten inches long. The bass hit a surface fly called a Sneaky Pete. I am not sure of the fly's size, but looking back, I believe it was around size eight. The fish was in shallow water near the bank, which is good, because I couldn't cast far.

I still remember the first trout I caught on the rod. It was at what is now known as Otter Creek Outdoor Recreation Area but was still Otter Creek Park back then. The fly I was casting was a black Wooly Bugger. I mistakenly called it a Wooly Booger; That was around a size eight. I did not know how to retrieve it. Drifting freely downstream, it neared the limbs of an uprooted sycamore. I stripped the fly in to keep it from getting tangled. As I did so, a sudden jolt awakened me from whatever daydream I was enjoying and I quickly landed a twelve-inch, stocked rainbow.

My favorite memory is my first trout on a dry fly. It happened at a small stream not far from Mammoth Cave National Park. I hadn't yet caught a trout on a dry fly, but all the books I'd read about fly fishing made it clear, catching a trout on a dry fly was of utmost importance. Yes, I was going to release the fish, and yes, the trout had grown up on trout chow in a fish hatchery, but this was still a big deal.

I had decided to fish the entire section of the trout-stocked stream, which I would guess to be around one mile long. Usually, I fished either the upper stretch near the small parking area, or the lower stretch, accessible from a side road. The stream was all mine since it was a weekday morning and since I hadn't ventured too far in either direction in the past; I planned to explore. Early on, I managed to catch a few trout using a Beadhead Pheasant Tail Nymph under a strike indicator. I rounded a bend and noticed on the upstream end across the creek there was a gravel bar that was the perfect place to stand and cast to the generous head of water that was flowing downstream. At the edge of the fast water, here the creek made an abrupt dogleg left, and at the edge of that turn, the current slowed. I decided to try a dry fly. I rummaged through my meager selection of flies and decided on a size 14 Parachute Adams.

A Parachute Adams is an attractor fly. It is not tied to imitate a particular species of aquatic insect. It just looks buggy. Therein lies its secret. It can imitate a variety of flies. The white wing post also makes it easier to see on the water. My first two casts didn't land at the edge of the current as I'd have liked. They were ignored. The third cast drifted right across the sweet spot and a twelve-inch rainbow smashed the surface and devoured the Adams. It was exciting. I subdued the trout rather quickly and while he was resting in my net, I admired the coloration of the fish. It had an olive back, with a faint pink stripe down the middle, and a silvery underside that faded to pearl white. The rainbow had small black spots on its back, fins, and tail.

It was a fine fish and though I had a long way to go, I was beginning to feel like a fly angler. This was big medicine.

By sheer chance, I learned there was a small fly fishing shop in Louisville, and I checked it out. I already had the budget-friendly fly rod and reel and a minuscule collection of flies, most of which were unknown to me. Despite my lack of casting skills, I still managed to catch some fish on my fly rod. Finally, I had a time to kill and found my way to the fly shop, which was tucked in behind a sporting goods store that catered to mountain bikers, canoe and kayakers and backpackers. It turned into an expensive visit. After finishing my shopping, I made three trips to my car to load all my new gear. I had a new, nine-foot, six weight rod and reel, a fishing vest, a few dozen flies in various patterns, colors and sizes, and a pair of Orvis waders.

I threw myself into the sport, devouring everything I could, such as videos, instruction manuals, and magazines. I started reading books about the sport. Some were instructive, written by guys like Lefty Kreh. Many of them, the ones I enjoyed best, took a more philosophical approach to the sport. The authors seemed to infer that there were deeper meanings to fly fishing than just catching fish. Guys named Gierach, Leeson, Maclean, Traver, and McGuane wrote these books. I bought a book at the fly shop by a guy named Schwiebert. It was all about bugs and was confusing to me because I don't know Latin. I also took a casting lesson (It was worth the money). Before long, I was becoming a competent fly fisherman, or at least I was catching more fish on a fly rod.

Nearly three decades later, I am still in love with the sport. I now fish often, and I am usually accompanied by my wife Jennifer. Over three decades later we are still enjoying life together, with kids and grandkids now. Even today, I can still remember that warm October night on her front porch and that first awkward kiss. Unfortunately, I still can't recall that first fish.

CHAPTER 3

DON'T GET CAUGHT
WITH YOUR WADERS DOWN

It was an unseasonably hot May morning in the foothills of the Great Smoky Mountains National Park. According to the radio, it was already 77 degrees, with an expected high in the mid-80s. This was the beginning of a hot, dry summer that would lead to drought and forest fires in the area. Eventually one would spread from the national park into the town of Gatlinburg, causing the loss of life, destroying homes and businesses, and triggering a mandatory evacuation of the area.

While driving into the park that morning, checking out the scenery through the windshield, I recall thinking that there was still plenty of water in the streams and the fishing was in full swing. Looking out at the ancient, round-shouldered mountains and their diverse species of plants and wildlife never gets old to me. These mountains are a part of me and although it was already steamy outside, I ignored the humid climate that causes the grayish mist that these mountains are named for.

The temperature would not have felt so bad had there been a pleasant breeze drifting down from the higher elevations, but it was not to be. Instead, the humidity was slightly suffocating, and I was forced to turn on the Durango's air conditioning. After I arrived at the Sugarlands Visitor Center, where I would meet my husband-and-wife clients for the day, I hoped it would be cooler in the higher elevations. It was already hot enough that I worked up a sweat while assembling and rigging the fly rods.

Bill and his wife Brenda, experienced anglers from Missouri, had not yet fished the small streams in the southern Appalachians. Bill explained to me their goal was to learn as much as they could about fishing these streams, so they could spend time on their own, fishing in the area. This is as close to perfect clients as you can find.

I took the couple to the Elkmont area of the park. The fishing there had been good lately, plus there is a lot of history around Elkmont and I enjoy explaining about the old railroad and logging village, and how the area became a weekend getaway for the financially elite people from Knoxville and other southern towns.

A few old houses remain standing in Elkmont, and people can rent the restored Appalachian Clubhouse for weddings and other events during certain times of the year. The Little River Trail parallels the stream for much of its journey and provides easy access for anglers. The trail is easy walking because it follows the original railroad bed that was used to remove timber from the area when the Little River Lumber Company was in business.

Elkmont, like much of the Smokies, has an array of trees. Oak, Beech, tulip poplar, hemlock, mountain laurel, rhododendron and flame azalea are prevalent throughout. The East Prong of the Little River flows through this section of the park and provides both rainbow and brown trout.

Elkmont is also home to a sizeable bear population. Nearly every run-in I've had with a bear, either while guiding or fishing on my own, almost always happens in Elkmont. I've had them cross the trail and creek where my clients and I are, had them pop out of the brush directly across the stream, and have even stepped off the trail to allow a sow with two young cubs to pass by; however, none of those encounters prepared me for what would happen on this day.

The day went exceptionally well. Bill and Brenda were good anglers that knew their way around a trout stream. They immediately picked up the line control to achieve a quality drift, which is the most important factor for success on these streams. We were getting into fish and having a good time. It was getting close to lunchtime, which consisted of club sandwiches, a variety of chips, and a selection of sodas and bottled water. I was ready to unpack the coolers and chairs, but my bladder had been protesting for several minutes. I sauntered over to Bill and said discreetly, "you keep an eye on Brenda, you two keep fishing, I'll be back shortly."

As I walked around a bend out of sight, next to a rhododendron thicket, I unfastened my waders, unzipped, and let fly. As I was finishing up, I noticed the rhododendron shake. I instantly looked at the surrounding treetops, expecting to feel a bit of relief from the breeze, but all was still. As I glanced back down, the rhododendron parted, and a black bear head the size of a basketball poked through. I was 10 feet or less from this bear that was pushing 200 pounds. This is by far the closest I had been to the icon of the Smokies, and it was uncomfortable.

The National Park Service has a law that you should not be closer than fifty yards from wildlife. Through no fault of my own, I was much closer. Had a park ranger shown up, I would have been happy to see him and would have asked him to cite the bear for breaking the fifty yard barrier. Unfortunately, there was no one to help me.

I am sure I was quite the spectacle as I tried walking backwards down a rocky creek bank with my pants still unzipped, holding my waders up with my left hand and my bear spray in my right. The bear walked out of the thicket and stared. I was relieved that he showed no apparent signs of malice. I got back to Bill and Brenda, made myself presentable, and told them the story. They immediately walked around the bend with me and got some fabulous photos of the bear, who stood, sniffed the air, and then appeared to pose for the camera while making his way downstream. Every time I have peed in the woods since, my heart rate picks up and I scan all the brush.

This was not my first run in with a black bear. Once, while fishing the Rapidan River in Shenandoah National Park, a sow, with a pair of cubs crossed the creek upstream, paused on the opposite bank, left her cubs, and followed me at about 50-feet away until she successfully ran me away from the stream. I never felt in danger, but I knew that a sow with cubs was nothing to fool around with.

A more humorous incident happened on a guide trip, once again in the Elkmont section of the park. I was guiding a half-day trip with a father and his two grown sons. One son was an avid fly fisherman, while the father and other son had no experience.

The experienced son wanted me to give him an idea of where these fish live and then to be left to his own devices. I did that and within a few casts, he was into a small brown trout.

I kept dad and the other son together, spacing them in adjoining pools and leapfrogging each other as we moved upstream. As noon rolled around, I was in a predicament. Despite many opportunities—i.e., missed bites and fish that came off after being hooked—dad had not caught a fish. I really wanted to see him land a trout, and because this was my only trip of the day, I spent a little extra time trying to make it happen.

After gathering the troops, we moved upstream to one last spot where my clients almost always landed a fish. The fish there were usually not large, but they would attack almost any fly, provided it got a quality drift. So, I moved the son to the upper pool, perhaps 60 feet away, then began walking the stream bank back down to dad. I briefly visited the pool to survey the area and get him ready for his first cast. I finally sauntered over next to a large boulder that was half in and half out of the water. The rock was about waist high and offered a perfect ambush spot to hook and land a trout. As I motioned for dad to walk toward me, he got halfway there, stopped, and said simply, "snake." I glanced at the boulder where I was standing, where a copperhead lay sunning himself on the rock. I hurried out of striking distance of the venomous reptile, took a deep breath, and gathered my thoughts as the adrenalin let down.

While all of this was going on, we heard a shout from the son in the next pool. Unfortunately for him, we couldn't make out what he was telling us. We simultaneously yelled, "what?" Again, the son yelled, but once again we couldn't hear him over the roaring of the creek. After we let him know we still couldn't hear him a second time, he immediately began quickly wading out of the stream, while dragging a very nice TFO rod through the rocks and brush. When he finally reached us, he was slightly out of breath and flustered as he said to us both, "there is a bear, right f&%#ing there!"

Sure enough, a yearling male waded out of a stand of mountain laurel, came right to the stream edge, stared at us for a moment, then did an about face and ambled back the way he came. I thought it was a cool series of events; the father and son seemed to differ in that opinion.

Unfortunately, not all bear encounters in the Smokies end so well.

Glenda Bradley, a popular 50-year-old schoolteacher in Cosby, Tennessee, met her death when two predatory black bears attacked and killed her. According to the National Park Service, she was the first person killed by a black bear in a federal park or reserve in the Southeast.

Bradley, an experienced hiker, and Ralph Hill, 52, entered the park about noon. The couple, who had been reconciling, hiked about 10 miles from Gatlinburg. Hill told authorities he left Bradley on the trail to go fishing. He returned about an hour later to find her backpack on the trail and two black bears, an adult female, and a yearling, at her body about 50 yards away. The 111-pound adult bear apparently killed Bradley.

A nearby hiker summoned Park Rangers at the campground, and rangers eventually put the bears down. It was unclear to officials why the bears attacked.

"This was simply an unprovoked attack,' Phil Francis, the park's acting superintendent, said.

The final official report on the attack stated that two bears attacked Bradley, who was regarded as an experienced hiker in the Smoky Mountains, during a hike along the Little River Trail at the intersection with Goshen Prong Trail. Rangers with the GSMNP later arrived on the scene and killed both the sow and the cub believed to have attacked Bradley. It marked the first time in the history of the National Park Service that someone had died because of a black bear attack. The investigation and autopsy results confirmed Bradley died from injuries caused by a bear attack. They ruled the manner of death as an accident.

While wildlife biologists and park officials may never know exactly what triggered the bear attack on Bradley, they offer some observations that can help you stay safe in bear country. You can find this on the National Park Service website.

CHAPTER 4

MURPHY AND HIS LAW

"Many of us would probably be better fishermen if we did not waste so much time watching and waiting for the world to be perfect."

--- Norman Maclean

"Anything that can go wrong, will go wrong."

---- Murphy's Law

It was two days after Christmas when I drove into the Otter Creek Outdoor Recreation Area to meet up with a new friend and spend my last day of fly fishing for the year 2020. Seeing all the vehicles in the parking area should have given me a clue about how the day was going to turn out.

Darrell was a guy I went to elementary school with, and I played on a basketball team with his older brother, but we didn't really know each other. It was a chance meeting on social media that brought us together. Darrell had just received his first fly rod as a Christmas gift and was eager to put it to work. I was just ready to get out of the house and hopefully catch a few fish. I only accomplished one of these.

We hiked downstream about a half mile to one of my favorite spots. It's a place that rarely seems to have anyone in it. It is a wide pool with a good head of current coming in. A shelf drops off on the far bank, right where the current slows, and trout love to hang out right at the edge of the shelf. It is a great area to hook a few trout; most of the time.

As we were getting rigged up, I explained to Darrell the old fly-fishing euphemism that states that it's not about catching fish, but about being out in nature, enjoying the sunshine, the beautiful scenery, listening to the birds singing, etc. I then made an emphatic statement: "That's what people say when they can't catch fish."

The weather couldn't have been any better for a late December day in Kentucky. The high reached 57 degrees. It was quite a turnaround from two days before, when the temperature dropped to 14, the wind chill was one degree and it had snowed about an inch giving us the first white Christmas that my grandkids had seen.

I'm unsure about the fly I started with, but I remember fishing it under an indicator. I believe it may have been the dreaded Mop Fly, because I had just tied some for the first time. I know the next two flies I tried, because I wrote it down in my journal before I left the parking lot at the end of the day.

I switched to a size 18 beadhead Pheasant Tail nymph under the indicator and produced the same number of bites as I did on the previous fly. By now, an hour had gone by. I had nothing to show for it, other than my knot tying skills, and Darrell had a half-hearted strike.

We moved farther downstream to a couple more pools that usually fish well. I changed flies to a size 20 beadhead Copper John. A few casts later, I saw a decent midge hatch coming off. I rummaged through my backpack, checking seven fly boxes, and realized that my midge box was not with me. Later on, I discovered it on my office desk. I have no idea why it was there, but the way things were going, it probably didn't matter.

I stuck with the Copper John and missed a strike. Two casts later, I drifted over the same spot, got a strike, set the hook, and had a fish on;

for about five seconds. It would be the only action of the day. We finally moved down to my favorite area, only to find four other anglers fishing, and two standing nearby waiting. We spoke with them for a minute and called it a day.

Anglers may not like it, but getting skunked is a fact of life. It has been happening to anglers since the dawn of time. The difference now is that fishing is not a matter of eating or not, but it does wound the pride. Imagine in the days of our forefathers, Igor arrives back to the family cave where his wife berates him because he didn't bring any fish home to roast over the primitive family fire. His kids are shouting "thanks a lot dad, I guess we are stuck eating twigs and berries AGAIN!"

If you look at fishing from a philosophical viewpoint, you can even take some solace in the skunking. Fishing (and hunting) are enjoyable activities that stem from our hunter/gatherer heritage, but nowadays, achieving success is not as crucial as it used to be. In the end, not catching fish is not a big deal. Chances are, you were going to release those trout anyway.

Hiking back up the trail became a challenge because large sections of it were covered in mud, and it clung to my felt-soled wading boots. It had been a while since I last fished Otter Creek and it occurred to me on the hike out that they had made the trail longer and steeper since the last time I was here.

Once we reached our vehicles, I realized I had lost my net. This was not a big deal; except I wondered how I lost it. After all, neither of us used it to net a fish. The net was old, with faded wood on the handle and a rubber mesh basket that had seen better days. As I was removing my wading boots and waders, I took a moment to reminisce. The net helped me land fish in Kentucky, Indiana, Tennessee, North Carolina, Colorado, and Montana. Still, it was not a significant loss.

On the drive home, I relaxed despite not catching a fish. It happens, even to better anglers than me. It was still a good day. After all, it's not about catching fish. It is all about being out in nature, enjoying the sunshine, the beautiful scenery, listening to the birds singing, etc. At least, that's what I tell myself when I don't catch fish.

It may have started two days after Christmas, but it didn't end there. In fact, it continued through the early portion of summer. What is IT? My sudden inability to catch fish and have things go wrong on fishing trips. Things I've never seen, at least not this much. It started on my home stream. The stream where I caught my first trout over 25-years ago. I took a new friend on his first fly-fishing excursion, and we got skunked. Zero. Zip. Zilch. Nada.

It was one day, and even the best anglers can have a bad day. It wasn't the day I was hoping for, but there was a lot more fishing to do. Over the next few weeks, I would return to Otter Creek and catch plenty of fish, including one day when I caught around 30 in a three-hour trip. Still, there was more bad luck in store.

"*Cumberland tailwaters/Hatchery Creek bound. The need to cast a fly rod in a trout stream is reel (see what I did there).*" A Facebook post from May 27th. made just prior to leaving my house.

I was excited about an upcoming trip to the Cumberland River tailwater and the adjoining Hatchery Creek. I was excited about the trip, and it wasn't just for the fishing. There, I was going to meet up with a couple of old high school friends that I hadn't seen in a while.

Russ was a couple of years older than me, but we grew up in the same small community and he has a brother my age. In fact, his dad was my youth league basketball coach for a couple of years. Greg was also a couple of years older than me. He was in education, but his passion is basketball, so he went into coaching. He is now the head coach of a division one women's college basketball team.

Since I had a two-and-a-half-hour drive, I went down the day before to get a campsite nearby. This would also give me time to fish a little that evening before meeting Greg and Russ the next morning. It was not meant to be. After a quick stop at a local chain store to pick up some last-minute supplies, I jumped on Interstate 65 heading south. After just three or four miles, I hit traffic at a dead stop. It turns out, there was road construction, and someone had managed to have an accident in the construction zone. It would end up taking me two-and-a-half hours to go twelve miles. Twelve Miles!? I should have been setting up my tent by now!

I reached an exit, where I pulled off to make a sandwich, eat some chips, have a soft drink, and regroup. It was frustrating, and this is not the way to begin a relaxing fishing trip. While eating in the parking lot of a truck stop, I could see up ahead on the interstate and it looked like the bottleneck was over in three quarters of a mile. So, after finishing the rest of my roast beef and provolone sandwich, I jumped back on the Interstate and made my way through the traffic. It would be smooth sailing from here on out. I would still have time to set up camp and fish a couple of hours before dark.

"Not so fast, my friend." --- Lee Corso

Driving south on Interstate 65, I was able to cover about four miles before hitting another construction zone. Ugh. This was barely moving, but at least I hadn't come to a complete standstill. I thought everything was going to be okay, since I was almost at the parkway where I would exit off the interstate. Once again, I was wrong.

Over the years, I have made this drive hundreds of times, but it had been a few years. So why did I get off on the wrong parkway? I do not know, but I did, and it only added to my frustration.

I took the first exit off the parkway, pulled on to the shoulder, and pulled up the GPS on my phone. This would be a big plus, helping me navigate the back roads into the small town of Hodgenville, where I got on the Lincoln Parkway. From there, it was an easy, albeit slow, drive. I was traveling on a two-lane state highway until I reached Campbellsville. Once I got through Campbellsville, Columbia was close by. In Columbia, there is a particular red light in a curve, where I always get stopped. In hundreds of trips through here, I don't believe I have ever caught this light when it was green.

Once I got through Columbia, I felt like I was almost there. The highway stretches out until it meets U.S. 127 in Jamestown. From there, it's a short drive to my campground. Once I reached my destination, it was late in the day, with about an hour of daylight left. Upon checking in and reaching my campsite, I felt frustrated and disappointed once again.

"Worst camp site I've stayed in, in 54 years on earth. Hopefully the fishing is good tomorrow." Facebook post from May 27th.

As I pulled up to my campsite, I was crestfallen. Again. It looked as though the site had recently undergone some work, but I am not sure it was for the better. Mulch was spread all over the uneven ground. There was no flat spot anywhere, not even for the tent. The picnic table was drug back to the edge of the woods on a severe slope and the lantern post was on the same hillside. Not that it mattered, because I didn't realize that there were no mantles for the lantern regardless.

"Oh yay. Let's make things even better. I just realized I left my two pillows at home. I also left my three, pre-made hamburger patties at home. Luckily I had roast beef and provolone in the cooler. At least I remembered to bring bread. Oh yes, I also have no fire ring at my campsite and I found out, there are no mantles for my lantern. FML. My journal is going to be full of curse words at the end of tomorrow. At least I have a good cigar." Facebook post.

According to the weather forecast before I left, they expected the area to get pop up showers with light rain for both days. When I arrived, it was sunny and dry. That didn't last long. I made a couple of sandwiches, grabbed a bag of chips and a drink, and sat down to relax, eat, and then read some before I hit the sack.

***"And now it's raining. Ugh!"* Facebook post May 27th.**

It drizzled shortly after I sat down to eat. By the time I finished it had turned into a heavy downpour, so I ducked into the tent, laid back on my cot, using the sleeping bag as a pillow, and read *River Hippies & Mountain Men* by Patrick Taylor. I could relax and unwind with the book, knowing I was snug and dry as I listened to the rainfall on the tent. I still held high hopes for the morning.

***"Nice, I forgot to bring a coffee Cup."* Facebook post from May 28th.**

Yes, it's true. I forgot one of the important camping staples: a coffee cup. I improvised by taking an empty water bottle, cutting off the top section, and filling it with coffee. While on my second cup of java, Russ called, and we firmed up our meeting time and place. I began taking down camp and packing up the back of the little Jeep Compass. It began a steady downpour, so I stopped, pulled on my rain suit, and continued packing everything away. As I drove out of the campground for our rendezvous at the hatchery parking lot, the sun poked out, and it was glorious.

The oak, poplar, and beech trees were dripping rain in the bright sun. Occasionally, you could see the remnants of dead ash trees and stumps. The ash trees were infected by the Emerald Ash Borer, an invasive species that first arrived in the U.S. in 2002 and in Kentucky in 2009.

I pulled into the parking lot to find Russ and Greg already there. We exchanged pleasantries and Greg gave me a new T-shirt that represented his team, the Western Kentucky University Lady Hilltoppers basketball team, where he is head coach. I promised to wear it and attend at least one game this season.

After some fits and starts, we found a parking area with a trail to access the creek. Once on the water, we experienced missed bites, made many fly changes, observed a very pregnant doe, and landed no fish. The rain started about an hour after we got on the water, and for the next three hours, it would alternate between a slight drizzle and an all-out deluge. Of course, my rain suit was in the back of the Jeep, where I tossed it after packing up camp. Oh, and the Jeep was at least a mile away.

Finally, after four hours, we headed back to the parking area. Russ and Greg drove downstream some thirty miles to try fishing the tailwater. I gave up and lived to fight another day. I was tired, frustrated, and emotionally exhausted.

So, Greg and Russ left. I got into my Compass and made one last Facebook post before driving home.

***Rain all damn day. Screw you mother nature. Fishing is stupid, I'm going home!* Facebook post from May 28th.**

CHAPTER 5

ADVENTURES IN BROOK TROUT

It was a stunning late-April morning in the Smoky Mountains as I pulled into the parking lot of Little River Outfitters in Townsend, Tennessee. I was there to meet my friend, writer Gary Garth. We were going in search of brook trout in Great Smoky Mountains National Park, on a tributary of the Middle Prong of the Little River.

Gary was here to do a feature in the travel section of USA Today on trout fishing in the national park. I had just moved to the area and started guiding for a guide service in Bryson City, NC. I was going to show Gary around. We would fish together, and he would conduct interviews with various guides, fly shop owners, and park fisheries biologists. There was also one other stipulation. One of us needed to catch a brook trout for pictures to accompany Gary's article.

I don't know about others, but when the NEED for a fish for pictures arises, I can feel pressure right away.

Lynn Camp Prong is a small sample of a successful brook trout re-introduction effort by the National Park Service with help from local volunteers. Before the establishment of the national park, roughly 75% of what is now Great Smoky Mountains National Park was clear cut for timber. This eroded the stream banks and produced an overabundance of direct sunlight on the streams. This altered the habitat beyond what brook trout can survive in. Brook trout disappeared completely from most of the park.

To improve the fishing, some locals began bringing in rainbow trout from California. Those non-natives found the park's high-gradient, well-oxygenated waters to their liking. The rainbow trout flourished and filled the niche left by the brook trout. Later, limited brown trout stockings occurred until the 1970s, when the U.S. Fish and Wildlife Service and National Park Service began evaluating brook trout within the park.

The Park Service decided to preserve native species if possible. This put an end to the stocking of non-native rainbow and brown trout, and closed fishing in sections of streams that still held wild brook trout. They started intense restoration work after identifying the park's native trout waters. Above waterfalls, cascades, and other natural barriers in historic brook trout waters, the park authorities removed non-native species. They transplanted some of the native fish still swimming in the park into those areas.

Now, brook trout are readily available in several higher elevation streams in the park. Opportunities for brook trout angling range from streams that you can practically drive to, to creeks in the backcountry that take some sweat equity to reach. Gary and I elected to explore Lynn Camp Prong, which had opened to fishing the year before, after a seven-year stocking of the native species.

Now is where I insert the mandatory statement that brook trout are not true trout but are members of the char family. Nearly everything ever written about brookies mentions this, so I felt it important to mention it here. Obligation over.

Gary and I pulled off at the gravel lot where the trail starts. We rigged up with a dry dropper combination, with a size 12 elk hair caddis for the dry fly with a size 18 beadhead pheasant tail nymph about 18 inches below. I explained to Gary that the dry fly would basically be a strike indicator and that most of the bites would be on the smaller nymph below the surface.

As we approached the trailhead, we stopped on an old bridge and looked around. Deep woods with dappled morning sunlight surrounded us, with stands of rhododendron lining the stream banks. Three streams, Panther, Lynn Camp, and Indian Flats merge here and form the Middle Prong of the Little River. We followed the trail that paralleled the stream, eventually breaking through a patch of rhododendron and scrambled to a spot where the current funneled from a narrow ledge and spiraled into an indigo-tinted pool.

On Gary's second cast, a brookie flashed at the dry fly but was not hooked. This would happen to both of us a few times and every fish hit the dry fly. So much for my theory that morning. Eventually, I cut the dropper off, and we fished with dries the rest of the day.

We leapfrogged our way upstream and in about 15 minutes I landed the first brookie of the day, about 7-inches long, and that took the pressure off. The fish itself was beautiful. Along its sides, the brook trout's color transitioned from olive to an orangish red, with scattered red spots bordered by pale blueish haloes. The lower fins were orange, and each had a white streak and a black streak, and its underside was a translucent white.

While the fish was gorgeous, the fight and landing of the fish was not. While needing a fish for Gary's article was a necessity, the need to land one had me strung tighter than an over-tuned piano string. When the trout hit the dry, I uncoiled, setting the hook, and yanking the fish directly out of the water in an arc that would send it over my shoulder. I grabbed my leader as it was going past and kept the fish from landing in the rocks or arching into the rhododendron thicket just behind me. I looked at Gary and explained that the key was to land them quickly.

Once the photos were done, we continued to fish for the next few hours, landing a few more specks as the mountain folks called them. As mid-day approached, I dropped Gary back at the fly shop to get his truck so that he could get some work done. I introduced him to Daniel Drake, manager, and part owner of Little River Outfitters, which in my mind is as fine of a fly shop as you will find anywhere. Later, he would interview some park biologists, including Matt Kulp, the supervisory fishery biologist for GSMNP and a long-time veteran of helping manage park waters.

This was my first time catching brookies with a photographer, but it was not my first brook trout rodeo. I had caught these little native jewels in Virginia, North Carolina, and Tennessee in the past.

My first trip to target these fish was not very fortuitous. My late, younger sister Beth and her husband had moved to the Washington D.C. area so that my brother-in-law Sean could attend law school. They assigned me the task of driving a 26-foot moving truck, loaded with all their furniture and other belongings to the area.

It was on this trip that I knew my brother-in-law had all the qualifications for a talented lawyer. He lured me in with cash and the prospect of a quick trip to Shenandoah National Park, where I could enjoy a day of fly fishing. According to him, the drive from our Louisville home to Alexandria was a simple 10-hour trip. He was right if you were driving a car. It turns out that driving a huge, old box truck with a governor on the carburetor through the Blue Ridge Mountains makes it a 12- and one-half hour excursion, which gets exciting when you get to the Beltway during rush hour. He also omitted the fact that they were moving into a third-floor apartment and there was no elevator to help get the furniture to the third floor.

We spent the next day unloading and unpacking, but the following day, I was free to explore. My cousin Joe, who had helped with the move and kept me company on the drive, was along and we decided we would leave early and fly fish in the national park. We went to a local store and purchased non-resident fishing licenses and got on the road, under a gorgeous sunny sky. After arriving in the park and paying our entrance fee, we consulted a park map and planned the day.

We decided to hit the Rapidan River, a well-known brook trout stream that President Herbert Hoover used to fish after building him a personal retreat there during the Great Depression. After plotting our course, we spent the next two hours driving in circles and not finding where we wanted to be. We even somehow exited the park and would have to turn around and go back to square one. The attendant at the information booth recognized us upon arrival but wasn't sure where the Rapidan River was. After a couple of more times of stopping to consult our map, we finally got our bearings and located the stream. When we finally laid eyes on the Rapidan, it started pouring rain, along with thunder and lightning crashing around. It was a wasted day. We were getting on the road the next morning, so there would be no fishing on this trip.

As fate would have it, I would be back visiting my sister and her family. My wife and two children, along with my mom, were also on this trip. We spent a day visiting Washington, D.C., taking in the sites. We visited the White House, the Capitol Building, and took in a couple of the Smithsonian Museums. On our second full day, everyone else went back to D.C. and I took the car and headed back to the Rapidan to give it a shot. The weather was perfect - mild temperatures with just the right amount of cloud cover to make the brook trout interested. I fished a dry fly; I believe it was a small yellow stimulator, with a nymph on a dropper. The majority of my day was spent roll casting to areas that seemed promising, netting three or four brookies before a poor cast caused the leader to tangle (hey, it happens).

As I stood on the creek bank cutting and retying the leader, I caught movement out of the corner of my eye and froze as I watched a black bear with two newborn cubs cross the creek about 50-yards upstream from me. They didn't seem to notice me until the sow got across the creek and froze. She stood on her hind legs, sniffed the air, dropped to all fours, and made a loud woof. The two cubs quickly climbed the nearest tree as mom moved closer, I quickly retreated. This went on for what seemed like an eternity, but was probably about 45-seconds. Suddenly, a group of hikers coming down the trail saw me, then saw the bear. During their excitement to get close to me where they could get a better picture, they inadvertently spooked the sow, who quickly retreated across the stream to her waiting cubs. After she disappeared with her offspring, the hikers went back to their trail. I decided I had enough excitement for the day. I had caught enough brookies, had a bear encounter, and enjoyed some beautiful Blue Ridge Mountain scenery under a gorgeous sky. What else can you ask for when seeking adventures in brook trout?

CHAPTER 6

BOW HUNTING FUN

I can still remember it like it was yesterday, though it is going on 30 years. It was a balmy, Indian summer day, the kind that can bring a type of joy to the heart of an outdoorsman in late November in Kentucky. An almost perfect day to be afield with a recurve bow and a quiver of arrows.

I was with my father-in-law Danny, bow hunting a small section of land on the outskirts of a little Kentucky town. The Thanksgiving holiday had passed two days prior, marking the unofficial start to the late archery season. It was getting on toward lunchtime and my stomach was letting me know. I had been in the woods about six hours but hadn't seen a deer. I hunted my way back to the truck to meet my father-in-law and decide what we were going to do about food.

The plot of land we were hunting was small, probably around 20 acres. On the backside, a huge cornfield bordered the plot of land, while toward the front, the woods thinned and led to a small pond, where a hill gently rose and thick grasses and weeds covered it. This led to the bordering property, which was an operating tree nursery on which we didn't have permission to hunt.

I was following an old logging road which exited the woods a couple of hundred yards from my tree stand. I entered the field and as I was trying to slip quietly toward the truck, movement caught my eye. Not sure what I had seen, I froze in place. Scanning the tall grass in the field, my eyes finally made out the body of a doe. I immediately dropped to a crouching position. The whitetail was at least 60-yards from me, well out of range of the Bear recurve I was carrying. Getting closer was necessary.

As I moved through the weeds, I kept an eye on the deer, stopping occasionally to confirm the doe's presence. I eventually closed the gap to 25 yards, rose on one knee and took a clear shot through a lane in the weeds. My eyes tracked the flight of the arrow, and it disheartened me to see it land right under the chest of the deer. Disappointment and frustration overtook my mind. I couldn't fathom how I had missed that shot. My first, at a deer with traditional archery equipment.

The deer didn't spook. Instead, she simply walked down the hill toward the pond. I thought I knew where she would go. Thinking she would bypass the pond and make her way to her bedding area in a thicket on a slight incline. I also knew a way that I might cut her off. Swiftly, I found my arrow, inspected it for blood (knowing it wouldn't be there), then retraced my steps down the hill and found a spot near the pond. I had lost sight of the doe, but I was pretty sure she was heading my way.

I stationed myself 15 yards away from where I expected the deer's appearance. After a brief wait, I heard a rustling behind me. Glancing over my shoulder, I saw the deer, using a different trail, which was seven yards from me. I turned quickly and take a shot that landed angled behind the rib cage. The arrow buried deeply but didn't pass through.

The doe took off at a high rate of speed toward the thicket. At least, that's where I thought she was going. I backed out of the area and went to find my father-in-law. I showed him where I was when I took the shot, how the deer reacted, and which way it went. We took up the trail, which was easy to follow in the tall grass, but we didn't find a blood trail, which was disconcerting. We reached the edge of the pond near the thicket and split up. I went to check the thicket while my father-in-law walked along the edge of the pond. After about a minute,

I heard him shout. I made my way toward Danny, and he told me he had found some blood. I asked where and his reply was, "right here on her shoulder."

Not only did I provide meat for my family, but I also hunted the deer in the same way as my ancestors, which made me proud. Suddenly, I became hooked on traditional archery, even though I had a lot to learn. It would be three more years before I took my second deer with traditional archery tackle, but I learned a lot during that time.

As I write this, Kentucky's archery season for deer and turkey is less than a month away. I will be back in the woods with a new takedown recurve. My first-time bow hunting since 2015. Why the long pause? The simple answer is "life."

I began guiding fly fishermen in 2016, spending all my time in the Great Smoky Mountains National Park. In addition, that was the year my grandson began playing youth league football, which took up my weekends in the fall. He is now starting his sixth football season and I have not missed a single game. Now that I no longer guide and am back in Kentucky full time, I will have many opportunities to bow hunt.

So, I am starting over. From 3Rivers Archery, I bought a new bow and twelve arrows. My latest purchases include two new Ameristep hunting blinds, new camo, binoculars, and multiple other accessories. I have been shooting the new bow almost every day since June, finding some consistency and learning what my effective range is. I've researched three public land areas extensively. These are all within an hour from my home. Trail cameras can help, but I am a firm believer in having boots on the ground to figure out deer behavior and locales.

As the arrival of each archery season approaches, I find myself excited, on the edge with anticipation even though I know that I have handicapped myself by using traditional archery equipment, but I enjoy shooting traditional bows and can accept the possibility of not taking a deer. I can only hope I am up to the challenge. Plus, deer hunting provides more than meat. The memories made, the campfire stories that are told, also add to the fun of hunting.

It was the first weekend in October as four of us, my cousin Joe, his brother-in-law Rick, and Rick's friend Tim, loaded up two vehicles and headed to a wildlife management area an hour and a half away. It was a Thursday and air temperatures were cool in the mornings and evenings, and warm and sunny during the middle of the day.

Traditionally, Kentucky's archery season used to start on October 1st. It didn't matter what day of the week it fell on; it was always the first day of October. Now it starts on the first Saturday of September, but we held off on this trip, when temperatures are usually cool, and the first leaves are changing color.

The management area contains a variety of forested habitats, including upland forests that are dominated by white oak, tulip tree, sugar maple, black gum, scarlet, black oak, northern red oak, sassafras, shagbark, and mockernut hickories. Box elder, black walnut and hackberry with some black locust and black cherry dominates riparian forests along the river.

One thing we really loved about the area is that it has a free, primitive campground. The campground operates without a full-time employee, and it operates on a first come, first serve basis. The only amenity is a concrete block, two-seater outhouse.

Confession time. I didn't grow up hunting. There were very few members of my family that hunted. My grandpa Tipton did squirrel hunt occasionally, and I had an uncle who hunted deer, but lived in Indiana, and I didn't see him often. The first time I went hunting, it was to chase squirrel with the man who would eventually become my father-in-law. I was twenty years old. Danny was an avid hunter and still is today at 81 years old. He still gets a deer every season.

Once I started hunting with Danny, many of my friends asked me, "why hunting?" It was hard to explained, and I still can't put my finger on it. I knew I wanted to be close to nature as a participant instead of a spectator. I knew wild game was delicious, and organic as hell, but there was more. Now that I am a 56-year-old husband, father, and grandfather, if someone asked me why I want to hunt, I am likely to respond, "because I'm a grown ass man and I can."

We arrived at the campground around four in the afternoon. After setting up camp and putting things away, we took off on a scouting mission for the next morning's hunt. We did a lot of driving and looking around. Joe and I were together in my Jeep Grand Cherokee. Tim and Rick were in Tim's truck with a topper. They planted most of the fields in corn or soybean. They gave local farmers leases with strict rules about what and when they could plant and harvest. Any field that was planted in corn one year would have to be planted in soybean the following year.

It was a win-win situation. The farmers had extra land to raise more crops, and the hunters had food plots that would attract and keep deer in the area.

The first day was smooth, if uneventful. We rose well before dawn, had coffee and breakfast, and were off to the woods. We hunted until lunch time, met back at camp for lunch and camp lounging, and then went back to the woods to hunt until dark. Only one of us saw a deer that day. It wasn't me.

Saturday morning, we repeated our early routine. The deer didn't seem to move that evening either. We were hunting as the moon was coming into full, and we speculated the deer were turning nocturnal. The crisp early October mornings with the cool temperatures and bright sunny and partly cloudy skies felt wonderful in the fall woods. After lunch and some camp relaxation, we fortified our plans for the evening hunt.

I had set up a blind Thursday evening near the edge of a wood line that led into a field with a small pond. Oaks that were dropping acorns surrounded me. Down a slight rise from the oaks and the pond, about 200 yards away, was a thick stand of pines with some other trees. Some had fallen, and a distinct trail went through them. I suspected that was a bedding area.

Joe rode with me that evening. In the parking area, an old logging road started behind a gate. Joe's plan was to walk down the logging road, which ran east, looking for deer sign and try to find a spot to sit and watch. My blind was a short walk southwest of the parking area. We split up to head out. Before leaving, we agreed to meet at the Jeep at dark, and then we muttered something stupid as encouragement.

That evening, I finally had a deer sighting. A doe with a button buck meandered out of the pines, heading toward the field and the pond. If they stayed on the trail, they would pass within 20 yards of me. I grabbed my longbow and nocked a cedar shafted arrow and readied for the shot. The thoughts of fresh backstrap at camp danced in my head. When they got within fifty yards of my blind, the doe stopped abruptly, stared a hole through the blind and promptly changed her route, heading back the way she came. About thirty minutes later, it was too dark to see. I made my way towards the truck and spotted a deer. As I neared, I could barely make out a small rack in the darkness as he waved goodbye with his white tail.

I tossed my pack and bow in the back of the Jeep, cracked open a drink from the cooler, and waited for Joe. Thirty minutes later, there was still no sign of Joe. My first thought was maybe he had a deer down, or he was having trouble locating the parking area, so I pulled the Jeep over to the gate, turned the headlights on and blew the horn a few times. Still no sign of him. There was one other truck in the parking area, and I saw two hunters approach it, so I got out, made small talk, and asked them if they had seen a one-eyed bowhunter. They hadn't. They left, and I grabbed my headlamp and started down the logging road to search. I walked maybe a half mile down the road, hollering for Joe, with no results. Finally, I gave up. Not knowing what else to do, I headed back to camp to round up Rick and Tim so we could go search the area.

The problem I had on arriving back at the campsite was that Rick and Tim weren't back yet. I panicked a little. I sped back to the parking area, hoping that Joe would be there, with a story about a deer down we needed to get, or at the very least, that he had gotten turned around for a bit, but eventually made his way back. Alas, when I got to the parking area, there was no sign of him. I once again pulled the Jeep up to the gate, put the headlights on bright, honked the horn and yelled. Nothing but the sound of my horn and my voice echoed. I walked back to the Jeep, waited about fifteen more minutes, and went back to camp for help. Panic was setting in.

As I approached the campground, I noticed Tim and Rick pulling in and then spotted Joe making coffee on the camp stove. Once I expressed my shock at Joe being there and explained to the others what happened, we sat around the fire eating while Joe told us his story.

As he was coming out of his hunting spot and hit the logging road, he made a right. He should have made a left. He had walked what he estimated to be a mile or a little longer when he realized he should have been to the Jeep by now. Not sure if he should turn around and try to retrace his footsteps, he continued the way he was going and assumed he would eventually come to a road and perhaps a house where he could find out where he was.

After another hour, he came upon a farm field and could make out the house in the distance. He crossed a barbed wire fence and made his way across the field to the farmhouse. He approached the house a little cautiously because he wasn't sure if they would appreciate visitors, especially after dark. An older woman answered his knock, and I can only imagine the look on her face as she saw a guy in full camo, carrying a bow, and sporting a glass eye. Luckily, she was friendly and asked Joe what he needed.

His first question was to ask how far from the campground he was, and which direction he needed to go? He explained to her he had gotten turned around in the dark and was trying to find his way back to the campground on the wildlife management area. She informed him he was about seven miles away and asked him if he needed a ride.

When we all sat around the fire that night and heard his story, Joe was subject to a lot of good-natured ribbing. The best dig happened as we all got ready to get into our tents and call it a night. Joe needed to walk the 20 yards to the outhouse before going to bed. That's when someone asked him in a sincere tone of voice, "Joe, do you want to borrow my GPS?"

CHAPTER 7

THE OUTDOOR WRITING LIFE

"And that, I've learned, is how outdoor writers do it. They hunt, they fish, they wander around in the woods, and then they write until they drop. They never retire from doing what's in their blood," --- William G. Tapply.

I ended up pursuing a career in writing by chance. Following a career in writing was never my intention, and after almost 30 years of writing, it still amazes and surprises me to see my name on a story in a magazine or newspaper.

Once, in a large chain bookstore in Louisville, just a short distance away, I found three outdoor magazines in the magazine section. All of them contained articles by me. The urge to grab a nearby stranger and, in an excited voice, while holding him by his collar, exclaim, "check this out man. I wrote these!" Fortunately, I fought off the impulse and meekly walked away.

I did my first published piece on a whim. A group of my family attended a large outdoor show in Louisville and discovered a booth for a tiny, free monthly magazine. The magazine was all about Kentucky hunting and fishing. I picked up a copy and took it home. A day or two later, I read it cover-to-cover and thought to myself, "hey, I can write as well as these guys." I didn't know it then, but this was not a lofty goal.

This was in 1994. I wrote that first piece by hand in a notebook and my wife typed it up on her electric typewriter that she had from high school. After completion, I dropped it in the mailbox. This was before the proliferation of home computers and email, so it had to go in an envelope with a stamp and dropped at the post office.

Time went on and I had forgotten about it when one day, I went to the mailbox and there was the magazine with my article. A check accompanied it for $25. It wasn't much money, but I heard that the large regional and national magazines paid well. By gosh, I was a professional outdoor writer now. I took the $25 and had a small order of business cards made that proclaimed me as one. It was a year later, after I learned some things about the business and about proper writing style, before I realized just how bad that article was and the next few were not any better.

I also learned that a very large fishing publication was looking for short destination pieces. After hearing this, I went to a nearby bookstore to purchase a copy of the magazine. After arriving home, I thumbed through the magazine to the destinations section to get an idea of what they were looking for. Then I placed a long-distance phone call to the editor in charge of the section. Making my pitch by phone for an idea that I was sure would fit perfectly in their publication. I made the phone call because I was very new to the writing game. I had never heard of a query letter. The sales pitch worked, and I got the assignment.

The article was to be 200 to 300 words. It needed to be short, succinct, with a quote from a fisheries biologist, a quote from a local guide about the fishing, along with some information about accommodations and the guide's contact information. My assignment was simple, really. In the early 1990s, Kentucky Lake, which is ranked as one of the top largemouth bass fisheries in the country, at least by people who compile these rankings. I am not sure of the qualifications a lake, river, or stream is required to have until it includes them in this list. All I knew about Kentucky Lake was that when I fished there, we seemed to catch more fish than other places. The premise of my article was based on the influx of smallmouth bass. Locals knew that the smallmouth population had expanded, but many around the country did not. My article focused on the smallmouth and that is how I had my first byline in a national magazine. Thank you, In-Fisherman.

Feeling confident, but knowing I had a lot to learn, I enrolled in a journalism class at the local community college that me and Jennifer were already attending. This turned out to be an excellent choice. In Basic Reporting 101, I learned about general sentence structure as it relates to print media. I also learned about Associated Press Style, something I had never heard of. This class also led to me working on the student newspaper, where I became the news editor. It was a great learning experience.

I worked many jobs during this time. There were many construction jobs, from framing houses, hanging drywall, to being a laborer on a brick laying crew. At a baseball bat museum, I gave tours and talked about baseball, despite not being good at the sport or having made a bat. I expanded my freelance writing. I sent queries to many magazines, got many rejections, but also enough assignments that I didn't give up. One of the interesting things about writing for magazines is the lead time. You are generally writing on a six-month lead time. This means you could work on a spring turkey hunting article, or about early season insect hatches on a small mountain stream, in the fall, when that time has passed and yet is coming again. When the story finally comes out in print, you haven't seen it for several months, and you have moved on to other assignments. Once you finally get a copy of the magazine, it's like reading it new.

I was getting published regularly in local and regional publications, with the occasional assignment from a national magazine. I was feeling pretty good about myself, but truthfully, I could not support a family on my writing income alone. Jennifer and I talked and decided that I should continue my freelance writing. Her job as a registered nurse made up the difference. Plus, I was home to get the kids to school each morning, get them home from school, do homework, and get to ball practices and games. It worked out well, but sometimes money got tight, and we struggled. Still, she continued to support me, and things are good. So good, in fact, once at an outdoor trade show, I was in a booth for a magazine I wrote for monthly. I was talking to a gentleman, and he says, "so you get paid to hunt and fish?" I explain that wasn't exactly the case, but he was on the right track. He finally asks me what the key was to being an outdoor writer, and I responded honestly, "the key is having a wife with a successful career," which is a factual statement.

Writing does not pay all the bills, but there is money coming in, and I have gotten to fish in many states around the country, from the Midwest, the deep south, and the Rocky Mountain West. I have met a lot of interesting people because of writing. Some of them were genuine characters.

My dad used to give me grief over me not punching a time clock and I spend so much time fishing and hunting. One time, he gave me a title for my occupation. It left a powerful impression on me. I have thought about getting me a placard for my desk. It would say Tim Tipton, Bullshit Artist.

CHAPTER 8

FIRE

My first year of guiding in and around Great Smoky Mountains National Park was as enjoyable as I had hoped. After returning from guide school on the Bighorn River in Montana in late March 2016, a guide service hired me shortly after. I suspected this could be a major turning point in my life and my wife's. Our family was expecting a baby sister for our six-year-old grandson. We had never lived this far from our kids, who were now adults out on their own. We picked the Smokies for several reasons. Both of us had been vacationing there since we were young. We knew the area well. The kicker was in the distance. We were an easy four-and-one-half hours away from home and could visit often.

Our first few days of living in the foothills of the Smokies were a revelation. I woke up to learn that a helicopter that took tourist on sightseeing tours over the area had crashed in nearby Pigeon Forge the day before, killing five people. The next morning, they found an elderly couple dead in a hot tub at their rental cabin. Then, a poor soul from Alabama committed suicide by jumping off the Space Needle in downtown Gatlinburg. Jennifer and I talked about if we could have jinxed the place and maybe we should return home and forget the entire plan. Things were not good, and I think we both had a bad vibe or whatever you want to call it that makes you question your decisions.

We decided to stick it out and stay and see if things improved. I started guiding clients by myself in early May. I enjoyed being outside in the mountains every day and everything started going smoothly. We were glad we had made it through the early tragic days. Little did we know how terrible things would get just seven months later.

The drought severely impacted the area that summer, and when a fire erupted on the Chimney Tops trail, the situation was deteriorating. Initially, authorities charged two juveniles with arson, but they later dismissed the charges because of insufficient evidence. My wife and I had returned home to Kentucky that weekend to visit family and go to my grandson's football game.

On our way home on a Sunday, it was extremely windy. There were a few times it nearly blew my Dodge Durango into the other lane as we traveled south on Interstate 75. As we got closer to our home in Maryville, we could see smoke from the flames. If the wind came out of the east, we could smell the forest burning. Reports on the news made it sound like the fire was contained in that area of the park. Park fire officials set a containment boundary made of natural features which were expected to hold the fire. Unfortunately, that wasn't the case.

Winds up to eighty-five miles per hour blew embers into nearby Gatlinburg, one of the biggest tourist areas in the southeast. In addition, the high winds blew down power lines, causing even more fires to spread. Jennifer and I were in bed early, tired from the quick road trip. My guide season was over, and she didn't have to work until the following evening. I woke up around five a.m., made coffee, and turned on the news. I was so shocked that I woke Jennifer up and got her into the living room to watch the news with me. During the night, the fire had spread to Gatlinburg. Government officials evacuated the entire town. Unfortunately, some people didn't make it. It was devastating. We watched a cell phone video on the newscast. Two men took it as they fled their rental cabin in an area known as chalet village. Fire raged on both sides of the road. During the video, you could hear one man praying aloud and you could hear the fear in their voices.

The aftermath was horrific. The fires resulted in the tragic loss of fourteen lives, while 190 others were injured, with some sustaining severe injuries. Great Smoky Mountains National Park was temporarily closed by the park service for a month. It was quite the blow to the most visited national park in the country, and the tourist towns that surround it. The loss of life and property was the biggest loss, but the residents who lived and worked nearby saw their loss of income become a major hurdle. This is where the heart, toughness, and resilience really caught my attention.

Signs on various businesses in nearby communities were using the hash tag #Gatlinburgstrong to show support. Lots of people jumped in to help, none more than Dolly Parton. Dolly Parton, a well-known philanthropist, who was raised in the area and owns many businesses in Pigeon Forge, consistently supports various causes. She immediately organized massive fundraising to help displaced families. Her My People Fund donated $1000 per month to each family that lost their residence. In addition, after handing out the last payments herself, she surprised each family with an additional $5000. Her Mountain Fund would pledge at least $3 million more over the next three years.

After a harrowing three-week ordeal, the Sevier County Mayor announced that they had extinguished all fires in the area. As I write this, in November 2023 there are still lawsuits pending in the courts against the National Park Service. There is some good news.

The National Park Service has become more aggressive in case of a fire. Recently, the area was under drought conditions and a huge windstorm was breaking out. They effectively closed the park down on most major roads and evacuated campgrounds.

Just recently, a fire was going on Rich Mountain Road in the Cades Cove Area. The firefighters quickly contained the fire, ensuring that no one was injured. They believe that the fire was intentionally started based on all signs during the investigation, and they are seeking the public's help.

Once the national park reopened to the public, after the 2016 fires, Jennifer and I took a morning drive to see the damage up close. Some areas were hard hit, while others were untouched. In areas, particularly near the Chimney Tops trailhead, where the fire originated, the standing burned tree trunks reminded me of a graveyard. We drove all over the Tennessee side of the park, surveying the destruction. Someone had sprayed some type of fire retardant material in certain areas. After letting the sights sink in, I finally wondered about wildlife and, lastly, the trout.

After testing many of the park's waters later, I noticed the trout were still there. Maybe not as many of them as there used to be, but they were still in all the usual lies in backwater eddies, hiding behind midstream boulders and other places. I had a feeling things would get back to normal, when on our way out of the park, we had to slow down for a black bear crossing the road.

CHAPTER 9

THE JOYS AND FRUSTRATIONS OF GUIDING

When I first thought of becoming a fly fishing guide, it was more of a dream, not something that would ever become a reality. I was working at a small newspaper as the sports editor, and I also wrote an outdoor column once a week. In addition, I was also freelancing for some regional outdoor magazines. I went on that first guided fly-fishing trip and thought about my guide and his lifestyle. Here was a man that got up every morning, excited to go to work. He didn't punch a clock and waste away in a factory or an office; he was out there on the river, enjoying the fruits of nature and living life on his terms. At least that was what I thought.

In reality, it is a little different from that, but still better than other places where I worked. While the hours can be long during the season, which was roughly May through October for me, it can be rewarding. I also envisioned in my head that I was the trusty, backwoods, steely-eyed mountain man who could tell you about the wildlife, the flora and fauna, and the history surrounding Great Smoky Mountains National Park. If needed, I could save you from dangers in the backcountry. That was my thoughts, but reality was slightly different. Each day was different. Each client was different. Some days were full of aggravation, some days were funny, and most days were full of enjoyable people, beautiful scenery, and colorful wild trout. Now, reminiscing back, there are some stories that stick out.

The Stubborn Angler

Fly fishing in southern Appalachian streams differs from fishing in large tailwater rivers. If you have never fished with a fly rod in the small streams, it can be an adjustment. The problem is the folks that have so much experience they don't need to listen to the guide.

I once had a client who was in town with family and brought his two twenty-something year-old sons to fly fish with him. It was a four-hour trip. The boys were novices. They had done a little of fly fishing with dad over the years, but they were not as experienced.

The first clue I had that this could turn out wrong was when they pulled into the parking lot at the Sugarlands Visitor. As we all shook hands, dad scrolled through his phone to show me picture after picture of large fish that he had caught over the years, in all the famous rivers out west. There were Pacific coast steelhead from Oregon, huge, dripping rainbows from the Henry's Fork, or maybe it was the Madison, I can't recall. I figure this guy had fished every famous river in the western United States. He had over 40 years of fly fishing experience, as he reminded me many times that morning.

I took the trio to a small, scenic stream that gets very little fishing pressure. It is an area where two small streams meet, and it even has a couple of small islands where the streams split and then meet again just downstream. The area has a well-known hiking trail, and parking gets difficult at times. When you enter the creek from the road, the fishing is good right there, and this is an area with two islands and the stream splits and meets again, all in a two hundred yard area. On the back side of the lower island is a small side channel that is usually good for a couple of brook trout if the water is at the right level.

On the far bank, across from the first island are some pretty good holes that always seem to hold fish. If you go to the far left corner, there is a short trail that gets you up on the bank. The rest of the bank is about a three-foot drop. The stretch through there is not accessible for wading, because you would spook fish all the way through there.

I let dad have that section because he was more experienced. I got the two sons fishing, and they were catching fish at a pretty good clip. The next time I looked at dad, he was standing knee deep in the middle of the stream making long casts and spooking most of the fish. I explained this again, for about the fourth time. He took the easy trail out of the water and went back to fishing like I showed him earlier. A couple of hours went by, and the two young men were catching trout well. At least they were smiling and appeared to be having a good time.

Towards the end of the half-day trip, I moved the sons up to the area near the parking lot and we saw dad fishing upstream in the area I left him. It's important to understand that, if you don't use the side trail coming out, you can jump off a small, rocky area, about a three-foot drop. Although I've done it myself, I always recommend my clients to use the trail for safety. I saw dad heading our way and before I could say anything, he jumped rather than use the trail. I heard the very audible crack and prayed it wasn't his leg. That was not the case. It was his Orvis Helios II rod that he had just purchased and was using for the first time. The rod snapped almost perfectly in half. I would also add that I told him he should use the trail instead of jumping. Twice.

We Just Want to Learn to Fly Fish

One of the satisfying things about guiding was teaching clients that had a genuine interest in learning the sport. I loved teaching beginners that truly wanted to learn. Those were my favorite clients and I loved working with them.

One of my favorite trips involved a father, who we'll call Jim. Jim had just purchased a family vacation retreat in the area. He had plans for his wife, daughter and other family members could vacation in the

Smokies whenever they chose. When we met at the visitor's center that morning, he explained to me they loved to fish, but had never fly fished. They wanted to learn the basics of fly fishing these streams and Jim told me that both he and his daughter Crystal agreed that they just wanted to learn, and catching fish was optional. You hear that often from clients, but few of them really mean it. I believed Jim and Crystal meant it, but fortunately, we never found out.

I taught them the basic roll cast, showed them line control and how to mend line, tips on reading water, a couple of simple, but effective knots, and many other basics. They both got the hang of roll casting quickly and became more adept at line control as the morning went on. Crystal, a young college student, was a natural at wading, easing around boulders, learning to move slowly but effectively in the water. She was also turning out some nice cast, and she had good hand eye coordination. She seemed like a natural and had the advantage of youth.

At the day's end, they both told me it was one of their favorite days they had on the water, and I agreed. They both made my day easy, and they were amiable people, and it was honestly one of my more enjoyable days guiding. Before departing, they both shook my hand, with Jims's hand having a crumpled bill in his palm. After they left and I climbed in my Durango for the short drive home, I reached in my pocket and peeked at my tip. There was a wrinkled one hundred dollar bill. The day had just gotten even better. Unfortunately, not all days were like that.

The Canadian Clusterf@#k

Sometimes circumstances become out of your control and all you can do is put your head down and keep grinding. In the Philosophy of Stoicism, they would categorize this as the Dichotomy of Control, or DOC. In its basic form, DOC means you can only control things you have jurisdiction over, but there are other factors beyond your control.

In other words, you can control things such as your attitude, your behavior, and your reaction to situations. You cannot control the weather, if there is a good hatch of insects, if the fish or feeding, the level and speed of the water, or whether your clients really care if they fish. This really stuck out to me during a multi-client, multi-guide trip that a group of us did once.

The trip was a four-hour outing that didn't start until after lunch. The clients numbered 22 and nine of us guides would split them into groups, but they all wanted to fish in the same area. This was one of those business trip retreats that bosses often use to build camaraderie at the office. They were from Canada and every one of them I interacted with, including my two clients, were fine people. They had accomplished a great deal during their time in the Smoky Mountains. Their adventures included whitewater rafting, horseback riding, and hiking. On this day, they would go fly fishing.

I never found out what kind of business they worked for, and I didn't ask. Most people retreat to the mountains to get away from the mundane day-to-day office duties, so I've found it best not to ask. Three things I always stay away from are politics, religion, and work. It makes life more peaceful for everyone involved. After we split into groups and did some quick casting lessons, we strung them out along the only stream large enough to accommodate a group this large.

The difficulties started rather quickly. Out of 22 clients, only one had ever fly fished, and he told us his experience level was very limited. That was fine. All of us guides dealt with beginners regularly. Unfortunately for both us and our clients, the conditions were tough. It was hotter than normal. There had been a lack of rain in the higher elevations and the water was low. We didn't realize it at the time, but the area was in the early stages of a severe drought, which would eventually lead to the raging wildfires of 2016 which would burn countless areas in Great Smoky Mountains National Park, rip through the nearby town of Gatlinburg causing much destruction and death. According to the Associated Press, the fire killed 14 people and caused an estimated $2 billion in losses, including about 2,500 buildings that were damaged or destroyed. The fire started on less than half an acre in a remote section of the park during the Thanksgiving holidays, when the park had minimal staff. To say it was devastating would be a gross understatement.

Despite everything going against us, everyone in the group seemed ready to give it a try. It ended up being a trying day. And it was really no fault of our Canadian guest. There were the usual things, such as tangled lines, flies broken off, flies stuck in trees and bushes. This is a usual occurrence when fishing, but the sheer number of people we were dealing with amplified it. After about an hour, you could see the group losing interest. By hour two, most of them announced they were done for the day. Groups of two and three began to file out in individual parties. We explained that there were two hours left they had paid for. They didn't really care. Eventually, they ended up in a picnic area drinking from coolers of Canadian beer that they had brought along. They offered us beers for our trouble and tipped nicely, but it sure wasn't what one thinks of when fly fishing in the beauty and serenity of the Smokies.

Purple Heart Veterans

One of my more entertaining trips during that first season of guiding was taking two war veterans for a half-day trip. I was excited when I found out about the trip because I have a special place in my heart for these guys. I am the grandson of a World War II veteran and the son of a Vietnam veteran.

My veterans that day were a lot like I imagined they would be, but also a little different. Both were solid country folks, which I could relate with because of growing up in Kentucky and spending a lot of summers at my grandfather's southern Indiana farm. In other words, these were my people.

Both loved to fish but had no fly fishing experience. That was fine with me. I was confident they would catch on quickly. They did. As they donned waders and wading boots, I rigged up two eight-foot, four-weight rods. There was one awkward moment before we hit the trail to the stream; they wanted to bring along a small cooler of beer. Drinking in the national park is illegal except for picnic areas and campgrounds. With normal clients, I would have said no, but these guys were different. There were five purple hearts between the two of them. They had done a couple of tours in Afghanistan and Iraq. Both had been medically discharged from the service because of their injuries. My thought at the time was that these guys had fought for our freedom, including the freedom to visit the national park that made these rules. The cooler of beer was coming along, even if I had to carry it. I didn't think a ranger would stumble across us, and if he did, he would probably let it slide with a warning. If not, I would take the ticket myself. There are some things that can't be compromised.

We hit the short trail to the creek. The water was the perfect flow for what I thought would be best for the way I wanted to fish. I carried the two rods, and one of them packed the beer. On one rod, I attached a size 14 beadhead pheasant tail nymph, while on the other, I tied a prince nymph. Both were fished approximately 18 inches beneath an indicator. During my cast to show line control, a fish bit. I didn't set the hook, hoping that one guy could come back on our way out. I felt conditions were prime for a good day and I wasn't wrong.

Early on, each caught their first trout. Both were rainbows and over the next four hours, each of them landed three or four fish each, including one brook trout. The weather was perfect, with overcast skies and highs only in the mid-60s before we were done.

When I dropped them back off at their hotel, they tried to tip me, and I quickly refused. I explained about my dad and grandpa being combat veterans and how I appreciated their sacrifices. I also had to ask them why they didn't take me up on my offer to stay out longer. After all, the fishing was good, and we had glorious weather. One of them finally explained that they had a great time, caught more fish than expected, and enjoyed it thoroughly, but they had run out of beer!

CHAPTER 10

DREAMING

"Fishing is not for wealthy men but for dreamers,"
---Nick Lyons

I am a dreamer. My wife, my kids, and grandkids, both of my parents, and many schoolteachers can attest to being frustrated by my habit of drifting off instead of paying attention. I've been this way for as long as I can remember. As a young man, my daydreams usually revolved around sports, but as I aged, it was mostly members of the opposite sex, along with sports.

When I got older and started dedicating most of my free time to fishing, hunting, camping, canoeing, kayaking, and other outdoor pursuits, I dreamed about these things. I still do.

One example of this occurred during a routine medical procedure. When the anesthesiologist was about to put me under, she said, "think positive thoughts" and my brain immediately went fly fishing. When the quick procedure ended and I woke up, I was pretty upset. I was fishing the Henry's Fork in Idaho. There was a heavy mayfly hatch on, and big rainbow trout were looking up. I might be the only person that wished a colonoscopy took longer. I really wanted a shot at hooking one of those big rainbow trout.

Now that I am closer to 60, than I am to 50, a lot of my hunting and fishing has changed. I have started hunting almost strictly with traditional archery equipment. My hunting gear, most notably my recurve bow along with my quiver and backpack, are a mainstay in my truck. Besides my archery gear, I usually have a few fly rods and fly boxes along for the ride. This keeps me ready for any short-notice opportunity that presents itself. I have friends that hunt and fish in different ways than I do, who ask me why I choose such simple, outdated gear. I don't always think of an answer, but I think it comes down to simplicity and challenge.

There is something about challenging yourself with, as the kids now call it, old school gear. Sometimes we fish and hunt in more challenging, less productive ways. Why do we do this? Some say it is to test ourselves, to make success better appreciated. I have thought about this along mountain trout streams, while sitting in a deer blind, and even while sitting alone in my camper early in the morning, drinking coffee and watching the weather forecast. I have yet to come up with a definitive answer, but I know it is about more than fish. If catching fish is the only point, you might as well get a nightcrawler, a bobber, and some split shot and get busy.

In today's world of modern equipment and technology, it is easy to lose the joy you once had when you first fished and hunted. Just take fishing for example. With modern electronics today, it makes an angler's job much easier. Forward facing sonar is all the rage, from the bass tournament pros to your local crappie angler. It seems everyone is eager to drop up to $3000 to catch a few more fish. If you watch someone using this technology, they will stare at their screen while working their lure through the water. I sometimes wonder why not stay home and play a video game. The two look similar. I honestly don't care how a person chooses to fish or hunt, but for me, too much technology seems to diminish the sport.

I enjoy the simplicity of a fly rod, a few boxes of flies, a landing net, waders, and wading boots. It often seems, the fewer gadgets I carry, the more I enjoy the outing. In the summer, I don't even need waders. Just give me a pair of neoprene wading socks and my wading boots and I will be happy. I will carry a small day pack and a fanny pack. The fanny pack will have a few boxes of flies, some nippers, a few spools of tippet, and some hemostats. The hemostats are used to remove tiny flies from small fish, not for smoking weed along a trout stream, although I am sure that happens with some people. I choose not to partake; I have enough trouble getting around on a stream and trying to catch fish, to give myself even more of a handicap. Plus, my brain is naturally addled enough as it is.

In the daypack, I will have a water bottle and a few survival supplies. Minimal stuff such as a small first aid kit, a filter to get water when my bottle is empty, and some emergency fire starter, such as waterproof matches, along with a lighter. If I am going to be out for most of the day, I will take along a freeze-dried meal, a backpacking stove to heat water on, and a few snacks.

I started carrying the first aid kit after I took a particularly nasty fall on a guide trip. My client, an amiable man from Oklahoma, had booked a half-day trip and was struggling to hook and land his first trout. It was a four-hour trip, but since I had nothing else to do that day, I was determined to stay longer to give him every chance to catch his first fish on a fly rod. As we moved upstream to the next pool, I spotted a bear coming down. I pointed him out to my client, and we watched as it crossed the creek and headed back into the trees. My client was excited and suddenly got his second wind. Shortly after, he caught a brown trout, the first wild trout that he had laid eyes on. We called it a day. He was excited about catching his first wild trout and was, as he said, "stoked" to see his first black bear in the wild.

As we were getting ready to come out of the water, I took a misstep, lost my balance on a slippery rock, and took a pretty serious tumble into the water. I remember distinctly holding the fly rod high in the air to protect it when I went down. I cracked my shin hard, and it was swollen by the time I got to the truck I didn't know if I had broken anything, but after dropping my client off and saying our goodbyes, I stopped at a store on the way home and bought some Ibuprofen to try relieving the pain. When I finally got back home, my wife, who is an emergency room registered nurse, examined it, and declared that I was going to be on my way to the E.R.

I discovered that my left tibia (shin bone) had a deep bone bruise, but there was no fracture. That was not a big deal, but I had a cut on the shin, and wading without waders for the next two days got it infected. It remained swollen, and now red streaks appeared around the cut. I was running a fever by the time I finally got home, so my wife loaded me up and drove me back to the hospital. The cut had gotten infected from wading the creeks and developed cellulitis. I was given an IV antibiotic and sent home with an antibiotic prescription and ordered by my personal nurse to wear waders while fishing. All of this because I was dreaming when I should have been paying attention to where I was putting my feet.

There is nothing wrong with being a dreamer, bone bruise and infection aside, but you also must be a realist. There are things that you hope to do…. like catching an extra-large brown trout on a dry fly, and things that you realize are probably out of reach……like seeing Led Zeppelin live singing Stairway to Heaven. What you realize is that life and fishing are a lot alike. Some goals, while unlikely, are still attainable, while others are not. It's important to accept reality while keeping your dreams alive. It comes easily to a dreamer.

ABOUT THE AUTHOR

Timothy E. Tipton published his first outdoor article in 1994. He purchased his first fly rod in 1996 and has never looked back.

His work has been published in many magazines, including In-Fisherman, Bassmaster, Bass Angler, Bass Fishing, Cabela's Outfitter Journal, Kentucky Outdoors, Kentucky Afield, and many other regional and national magazines and newspapers.

With a background as a former professional boxer, he has held various jobs, such as a construction worker, a museum tour guide, a sports editor/writer, an employee at a fly fishing shop, and a fly fishing guide.

Currently, he works as a full-time freelance writer.

Tipton and his wife Jennifer have been married 35 years. The couple has two children, four grandchildren, and a bonus grandson. They live in a camper, and you can find it near a river.

Made in the USA
Columbia, SC
07 January 2025

49185996R00045